CW00591819

Antigua Travel Guide 2023

Embracing History, Culture and Adventures

Ted Dickinson

Table of contents

Introduction to Antigua, Guatemala

Chapter 1: Making Travel Plans for Antigua

Chapter 2: Getting to Know Antigua

Chapter 3: Accommodations in Antigua

- Best Places to Stay in the Area
- Upscale inns and resorts
- Affordable Accommodations
- Stylish Boutique Hotels

Chapter 4: Antigua's Dining and Culinary Scene

- Traditional foods from Guatemala
- Foods You Must Try in Antigua
- a restaurant or a cafe
- Sweets from the Street

Chapter 5: Outdoor Activities and Adventure: Exploring Guatemala's Natural Beauty

- Possibilities for Hiking and Trekking
- Volcano Climbing and an Overnight Hike in Acatenango

Chapter 6: Immersion in Cultural and Artistic Experiences

- Visiting regional galleries of art
- Traditional Workshops and Crafts
- Calendar of Festivals and Events 2023

Chapter 7: Entertainment and Nightlife

- Pubs and bars
- Live Music Locations
- Clubs at night and dancing

Chapter 8: Relaxation and Wellness

- Centers for meditation and yoga
- Wellness retreats and spas
- The Increasing Popularity of Relaxation and Wellness Techniques

Chapter 9: Practical Travel Advice

- Security and Safety
- Medical and Health Information

- Local Customs and Etiquette
- Green Travel Advice

Chapter 10: Day Trips from Antigua: Discovering Guatemala's Diverse Beauty

- Where Modernity Meets Tradition in Guatemala City
- The Pearl of the Guatemalan Highlands is Lake Atitlan
- Market in Chichicastenango: A Rainbow of Colors and Traditions

Language & Phrases Guide for Daily Use

Conclusion

Copyright © by Ted Dickinson 2023. All rights reserved.

Before this document is duplicated or reproduced in any manner, the publisher's consent must be gained.

Therefore, the content within can neither be stored electronically, transferred nor kept in a database.

Neither in part nor in full can be scanned, copied, faxed, or retained without approval from the publisher or creator.

Introduction to Antigua, Guatemala

Greetings from Antigua

Antigua is a charming city that oozes historic beauty and a rich history. It is tucked away among the magnificent highlands and volcanoes of Guatemala. Travelers are drawn to Antigua because of its cobblestone walkways, gorgeous architecture, and lively culture, making it one of Central America's most enticing locations. A gateway to Guatemala's interesting history, this charming city in the country's central highlands provides a lovely fusion of ancient Mayan tradition and Spanish colonial influence.

The well-preserved Spanish Baroque architecture of Antigua is famed for its vibrant façade, massive churches, and opulent mansions. Due to its small size, the city is ideal for sightseeing on foot so that tourists may really experience the culture. Every tourist may find something to enjoy in Antigua, whether they choose to wander through crowded markets, visit art galleries, indulge in wonderful local food, or just take in the breathtaking views of the surrounding volcanoes.

A Synopsis of Antigua's History

When Spanish conquistadors founded Antigua as Santiago de los Caballeros in 1543, it began to have a history in the 16th century. It quickly rose to prominence as the colonial capital of Guatemala and the seat of the Spanish Kingdom of Guatemala, which included the present-day nations of Guatemala, Belize, Honduras, El Salvador, Nicaragua, and Costa Rica, thanks to its advantageous location sandwiched between three massive volcanoes, Agua, Fuego, and Acatenango.

Antigua developed as an important center of trade, the arts, and culture throughout the colonial period. Its magnificent architecture, which mirrored the affluent era, showed its majesty. The heyday of Antigua, nevertheless, was not meant to remain. A series of severe earthquakes that rocked the city in 1773 left a path of devastation in their wake. Following this catastrophic tragedy, the Spanish Crown chose to move the capital to what is now Guatemala City, leaving Antigua in ruins.

Many of Antigua's colonial structures survived the earthquakes despite suffering substantial damage, and because to restoration efforts, the city was recognized as a UNESCO World Heritage Site in 1979. Today, wandering through Antigua's streets is like traveling back in time, thanks to the city's charming colonial architecture, which serves as a living reminder of its storied history.

Why Travel to Antigua in 2023?

Cultural Holidays and Customs

In 2023, travelers will get the chance to experience Antigua's celebrated lively cultural festivals and customs firsthand. The Semana Santa (Holy Week) festival, which is regarded as one of the most complex and dramatic religious spectacles in the world, is an example of this. The streets come alive with vibrant processions, complex sawdust carpets, and serious religious events throughout this week, drawing tourists from all over the world. The Feria de Santo Tomas, a vibrant festival held in December, also offers a glimpse into the local way of life by showcasing traditional Guatemalan dance, music, cuisine, and handicrafts.

Unparalleled Landmarks and Architecture

As previously indicated, Antigua is home to a wide variety of gorgeous architecture, from imposing cathedrals to admirably maintained colonial dwellings. The city is home to well-known structures including the Santa Catalina Arch, which serves as the city's emblem and provides spectacular views of the nearby volcanoes. The magnificent La Merced Church, an outstanding example of Spanish Baroque architecture with delicate façade work and holy relics, is another must-see location.

Outdoor activities and natural wonders

In addition to its historical appeal, Antigua has a variety of outdoor activities and breathtaking natural features. Trekking up adjacent volcanoes like Pacaya or Acatenango, where people may see breathtaking lava flows and panoramic vistas, is a challenging option for hikers. Tours of coffee plantations that include coffee tastings give visitors a glimpse into Guatemala's famed coffee culture. Hot springs and spas nearby provide the ideal chance to unwind and revitalize for those seeking tranquility.

Crafts and the Arts

The vibrant arts and crafts culture in Antigua gives visitors the opportunity to pick up one-of-a-kind keepsakes and support regional creators. Intricate textiles, handwoven fabrics, ceramics, and exquisite jade jewelry are among the traditional Guatemalan crafts on display at the city's many galleries and artisan markets.

gastronomic delights

The varied cuisine of Antigua will satisfy foodies. There are several eateries and street sellers around the city selling a broad variety of delectable foods that combine regional Mayan tastes with Spanish and other influences. Foods like Pepián (a robust pork stew), Kak'ik (a fiery turkey soup), and Rellenitos (sweet plantain and bean pastries) are popular among tourists in Guatemala.

In conclusion, Antigua, Guatemala, is a fascinating travel destination that fascinates tourists with its deep history, magnificent architecture, colorful festivals, and unspoiled landscape. Whether you are an adventurer, a history buff, or just a tourist searching for a real taste of local life, Antigua has something special to offer. 2023 is the perfect year to visit this unique treasure in the middle of Central America because of its retained colonial charm and wealth of activities.

Chapter 1: Making Travel Plans for Antigua

The lovely Caribbean island of Antigua is a top choice for tourists looking for beach, sun, and a lively culture. Antigua has much to offer every kind of tourist with its beautiful beaches, historical monuments, and pleasant environment. To visit this paradise, however, needs meticulous preparation that takes into account a number of variables, including the ideal time to go, transportation options, visa requirements, financial considerations, and language barriers. We will go into detail about each topic in this extensive guide to assist you in creating the ideal Antigua vacation.

Ideal Season to Visit

Climate and Weather
Antigua has year-round warmth and sunlight because to its tropical environment. When the weather is dry and nice, between December and April is normally when tourism peaks. The best range of daytime temperatures for outdoor activities and beach exploration is 25°C to 30°C (77°F to 86°F). There is a rainy season on the island from June to November, with the possibility of sporadic storms in the latter months. During this time, travelers should be

wary of weather predictions and think about purchasing travel insurance.

Events and Festivals
Antigua's lively festivals and events bring its cultural diversity to life. One of the most well-known is the Antigua Sailing Week, which takes place in late April or early May and attracts sailors from all over the globe for exciting regattas. Another highlight is the carnival, which has vibrant parades, local music and dancing, and is held in late July or early August. If you want to fully experience Antiguan culture, think about basing your travel schedule around these exciting occasions.

Accessing Antigua

air travel to Antigua
Major international airports are easily accessible from Antigua's V.C. Bird International Airport (ANU). Direct flights are provided by a number of carriers from North America, Europe, and the adjacent Caribbean islands. It is suggested to purchase tickets in advance, particularly during the busiest travel

times of the year since airline availability may change depending on the season.

Cruise vessels
Consider using a cruise ship to reach Antigua for a distinctive travel experience. You may take in the picturesque splendor of the island from the water thanks to the fact that Antigua is a port of call for several well-known cruise companies.

Entry requirements and Visas

Visa requirements
For entry into Antigua, certain nationals may need a visa. Checking the visa requirements unique to your nationality well in advance is crucial. Current information on visa requirements may be found on the Antigua and Barbuda Department of Immigration's official website.

Requirements for entry
Most travelers need a passport that is valid for at least six months after the date of entrance in order to enter Antigua. A return or onward

ticket and evidence of adequate finances for their stay are also required of passengers. When you arrive, immigration authorities could also ask why you are there.

Money and Currency Issues

Currency
The Eastern Caribbean Dollar (XCD) is Antigua and Barbuda's national currency. The US Dollar (USD), however, is commonly accepted on the island, and many establishments also accept major credit cards.

ATMs and other banking services
In large cities and popular tourist destinations, ATMs are easily accessible and provide a handy means to withdraw local money. Typically, banking hours are from Monday through Thursday from 8:00 AM to 2:00 PM and from 8:00 AM to 4:00 PM on Friday.

Gratuities and Service Fees
Antigua does not have a tipping policy, however it is typical to leave a gratuity in restaurants, particularly if service costs are not included, of

around 10% to 15%. Check before tipping since some hotels could add a service fee to your bill.

Speaking and Interaction

Governmental Language
English is the official language of Antigua and Barbuda. Communication should thus be rather simple for tourists who know English.

Local Slang
Although English is widely spoken, you could hear residents using Antiguan Creole, a vibrant dialect with influences from West Indian, British, and African languages. Your cultural experience will surely be enhanced by interacting with the locals.

To guarantee a seamless and enjoyable experience, careful consideration of a number of elements is required while planning your trip to Antigua. The ideal time to go, travel alternatives, visa needs, money issues, and language communication are all crucial considerations. You'll be ready to discover the magnificent beaches, ancient landmarks, and dynamic culture that Antigua has to offer if you equip yourself with this knowledge and do careful study.

Chapter 2: Getting to Know Antigua

Travelers from all over the world are drawn to Antigua, a UNESCO World Heritage Site in Guatemala's Central Highlands. It is a charming city with a fascinating history and beautiful architecture. A unique fusion of

Mayan and Spanish elements can be seen in this colonial jewel's well-preserved ruins, opulent cathedrals, and bustling marketplaces. We will explore the main tourist destinations, undiscovered jewels, off-the-beaten-path locations, enticing marketplaces, and souvenirs that make traveling Antigua an amazing experience in this book.

Top Attractions for Tourists

Arch of Santa Catalina

The Santa Catalina Arch, a charming stone archway that crosses 5th Avenue North, is one of Antigua's most recognizable features. It was first constructed to link the Santa Catalina convent to a school, but now it represents the city's rich heritage and colonial appeal. For panoramic views of the surrounding volcanoes and the city, visitors may climb up the arch, making it a must-see location for both history and photography fans.

Church of La Merced

La Merced Church is another magnificent structure that shouldn't be overlooked, with its spectacular Baroque exterior and beautiful stucco work. The church, which was built in the 18th century, has a tranquil courtyard and an excellent collection of religious art within. Visitors may see stunning panoramas of the city and its lovely surrounds by ascending the church's bell tower.

The Crucifixion Hill

Cerro de la Cruz provides a satisfying experience for hikers and nature enthusiasts. A short distance from the city center, this peak provides panoramic views of Antigua and the three adjacent volcanoes, Agua, Fuego, and Acatenango. Visitors of all ages may enjoy the very simple walk to the summit.

Metro Mayor

The lively Plaza Mayor, located in the center of Antigua, is surrounded by vibrant colonial structures, including the well-known Palacio de los Capitanes Generales. This public area offers a wonderful chance to get immersed in the local culture, take in lively street entertainment, and meet residents and other tourists.

Guatemala's Antigua Cathedral

The Cathedral of Saint James in Antigua Guatemala, sometimes called the Antigua Cathedral, is a magnificent example of Spanish Baroque design. The cathedral was first erected in the 16th century, but seismic damage forced multiple reconstructions. Particularly beautiful are the exquisite carvings and sculptures on its front. Visitors may browse the many chapels, altars, and religious items within to learn more about the city's rich religious history.

Unknown Treasures & Off-the-Beaten-Path Locations

While Antigua's well-known tourist sites are undoubtedly fascinating, the city also has several lesser-known treasures that provide a more personal and genuine experience.

Cultural Center La Azotea

The La Azotea Cultural Center is a fascinating and instructive place that provides information on Guatemala's indigenous culture and coffee farming. Visitors may see a coffee farm, a collection of indigenous textiles, and a museum dedicated to Mayan musical instruments here. Regular seminars and demonstrations are also held at the center, giving guests a fuller appreciation of the rich past of the nation.

Ground Lodge

Earth Lodge is an eco-friendly hotel and restaurant located in beautiful green hills overlooking Antigua for a distinctive and off-the-beaten-path experience. It's a great place for anyone looking for peace and a chance to get away from the busy metropolis. Rustic cabins and treehouses are available as lodging options, enabling visitors to enjoy the outdoors in a cozy and ecological manner.

Hobbitenango

Fans of the Lord of the Rings will like Hobbitenango, an eco-lodge with a hobbit motif that is perched on a local hill. The accommodations are made to seem like hobbit holes, giving guests a quirky and enchanted experience. The lodge also has hiking paths and wonderful valley views.

Examining the markets and souvenirs in Antigua

The colorful marketplaces of Antigua must be explored in order to locate one-of-a-kind gifts to bring home as treasured keepsakes.

Market for Artisans

Visitors will discover a broad variety of handicrafts, textiles, pottery, and woodcarvings in the vibrant Mercado de Artesanias. It's a great site to get genuine souvenirs from Guatemala and to support regional makers.

Nim Po't Center for Traditional Textiles

Nim Po't should be on the travel itinerary of anybody with an interest in traditional Mayan textiles. Beautiful handwoven textiles created by indigenous women from several areas of Guatemala are shown in this cooperative business. The business wants to protect the nation's textile history and pay the weavers fairly.

Market of Antigua

The city's main market, Mercado de Antigua, is where inhabitants go to purchase fresh fruit, meats, spices, and other necessities. Discovering this market gives you a real-life look into Antigua's people' daily routines and the chance to sample some delectable regional street cuisine.

Finally, visiting Antigua is a trip back in time when Mayan culture, colonial architecture, and the surrounding natural beauty all come together to produce a genuinely enchanting experience. For visitors looking for both history and adventure, Antigua provides a variety of experiences, from the popular tourist sites to hidden jewels and colorful marketplaces. Antigua guarantees a memorable and enlightening travel experience, whether exploring its old streets, marveling at its architectural beauties, or immersing oneself in the local culture.

Chapter 3: Accommodations in Antigua

The lovely Caribbean island of Antigua is a favorite stop for tourists looking for beach, surf, and a diverse cultural experience. It is not surprising that the island draws tourists from all over the world with its beautiful beaches, interesting sites, and lively environment. Antigua provides a variety of lodging alternatives to suit every taste and desire, whether you're a luxury tourist searching for an opulent hideaway or a frugal traveler seeking economical but comfortable options. In this guide, we'll dig into the best areas to stay in, analyze affordable choices, look at luxury hotels and resorts, and highlight little boutique hotels that are full of personality and charm.

Best Places to Stay in the Area

English Harbour is a must-see area for history buffs and sailors alike, and it is situated on Antigua's southern shore. Nelson's Dockyard is a significant centerpiece of this region's remarkable maritime past. Luxury hotels overlooking the port are available to guests, offering breath-taking views and convenient access to historical attractions.

Jolly Harbour is a thriving area with a variety of lodging options, including beachfront villas and apartments, and is located on the western side of the island. The region is a great alternative for families and those looking for a more self-contained holiday since it includes a contemporary marina, a golf course, and a variety of restaurants and stores.

Dickenson Bay: On the northwest coast, Dickenson Bay is a fantastic option if you're seeking for a beach paradise. There are luxury resorts and boutique hotels tucked along the beachfront, and the region is home to some of Antigua's most stunning beaches. While visiting this region, take advantage of the breathtaking sunsets and quick access to water sports and beach activities.

St. John's: The nation's capital city is a hive of activity. It provides a range of lodging choices, from luxurious hotels to affordable inns. For a true taste of Antigua, stroll through the vibrant streets, check out the renowned St. John's Cathedral, and browse the neighborhood markets.

Upscale inns and resorts

Hermitage Bay is a secluded all-inclusive resort located on the island's western shore.

Hermitage Bay offers a quiet and sumptuous refuge for affluent tourists with magnificent individual apartments and direct access to a private beach.

Curtain Bluff: A five-star resort with stunning views of the Caribbean Sea, Curtain Bluff is located on a green peninsula on the country's southern coast. It guarantees an exceptional luxury experience with first-rate features including a championship tennis facility, aquatic activities, and gourmet eating selections.

Carlisle Bay: On the south coast, with views of a beautiful bay, lies this chic and modern resort. It's a great option for both couples and families looking for a luxury getaway because of the roomy apartments and family-friendly amenities, including a kids' club.

Island of Jumby Bay - Oetker Collection: Jumby Bay Island, which can only be reached by boat, offers the best private island experience. This resort is associated with luxury and isolation because to its exquisite rooms, top-notch spa, and delicious dining selections.

Affordable Accommodations

South Point Antigua: Located close to English Harbour, South Point Antigua provides up-to-date lodging at a fair price. Without spending a fortune, take advantage of the rooftop infinity pool and the breathtaking views of Falmouth Harbour.

For guests on a tight budget, Connie's Comfort Suites offers comfortable accommodations at a fair price in the center of St. John's. The convenient location makes it simple to visit nearby landmarks, businesses, and eateries.

Trade Winds Hotel: For a fair price, this lovely Dickenson Bay hotel provides guests with cozy accommodations and a welcoming ambiance. For tourists who want to stay near to the beach without paying a lot, it's a fantastic alternative.

The Catamaran Hotel offers comfortable accommodations and a laid-back atmosphere while overlooking Falmouth Harbour. The on-site restaurant is a popular among travelers looking for a good deal since it delivers delectable regional food.

Stylish Boutique Hotels

Rustic-chic villas with individual plunge pools are available at the Cocos Hotel in Antigua, which is perched on a cliffside with views of the Caribbean Sea. It is the perfect option for couples looking for a romantic getaway because of the cozy ambiance and attentive service.

Sugar Ridge Resort: Surrounded by lush greenery and offering panoramic views of Jolly Harbour, Sugar Ridge Resort provides chic rooms and suites. Two swimming pools and the Aveda Concept Spa add to this boutique resort's appeal.

Nonsuch Bay Resort: On the southeast coast, this small resort offers airy rooms and villas with breathtaking bay views. It's a wonderful option for those looking for convenience and excitement since it has access to water activities and a private beach.

The Inn at English Harbour is a boutique hotel with a touch of colonial elegance and charm that is close to Nelson's Dockyard. A tranquil and opulent ambiance is created by the beautiful grounds, private beach, and delicious dining selections.

Antigua offers a variety of lodging alternatives to accommodate a wide spectrum of guests. In this Caribbean paradise, guests may choose from pricey luxury hotels and resorts to affordable inns and quaint boutique hotels to discover their perfect vacation. Any of Antigua's top areas and lodging options, whether you desire a seaside getaway, a historical adventure, or a romantic hideaway, provides a great stay.

Chapter 4: Antigua's Dining and Culinary Scene

The picturesque colonial city of Antigua, which is located in the center of Guatemala, is widely known for both its delicious cuisine and its well-preserved architecture. The city's culinary sector has an exceptional blend of indigenous Mayan traditions, Spanish influences, and contemporary inventions, resulting in a symphony of tastes that enthralls both residents and tourists. The traditional foods of Guatemala, must-try meals in Antigua, well-liked eateries and cafés, and tantalizing street food treats that will surely make a lasting impact on your taste buds will all be covered in this article.

Traditional foods from Guatemala

Guatemalan food is a reflection of the nation's diverse cultural background, with tastes heavily influenced by Mayan, Spanish, and other Central American influences. The main ingredients of Guatemalan cuisine include corn, beans, chiles, and different meats. Making tortillas, tamales, and other traditional meals using hand-ground masa (corn dough) is one of Guatemalan cuisine's most recognizable features.

The abundant use of herbs and spices like cilantro, oregano, achiote, and pepitoria, which add to the distinct flavor profiles of the meals, is another characteristic of the cuisine. Additionally, regional differences in ingredients and cooking methods enrich and diversify the Guatemalan gastronomic experience.

Foods You Must Try in Antigua

There are a few delicacies you must taste while in Antigua that you must not miss:

a) Pepián: Often referred to as Guatemala's national meal, pepián is a substantial stew cooked with meat (usually chicken or beef), vegetables, and a special sauce thickened with crushed seeds and spices. Usually, the meal is served with homemade tortillas and rice.

b) Kak'ik: This fiery turkey soup, which originates from Mayan culture, is enhanced with local herbs and spices. It is a preferred option for festivals and special events because of the warmth and depth of the tastes.

c) Chiles Rellenos: This delectable cuisine consists of roasted poblano peppers that have been filled with a mixture of meat, veggies, and seasonings. After that, a little egg batter is applied to the peppers, and they are cooked till golden brown.

d) Tamales: A cherished local specialty, Guatemalan tamales are prepared from seasoned masa and stuffed with meat, sauce, and sometimes raisins and olives. They are first wrapped in banana leaves before being perfectly steam-cooked.

e) Rellenitos: For dessert, savor rellenitos, which are made of sweet plantains that have been mashed and filled with a flavorful black bean paste before being deep-fried and dusted with sugar.

a restaurant or a cafe

There are many eating alternatives in Antigua, from quaint cafés to chic restaurants, to suit every taste and price range. Here are some excellent suggestions:

a) Café Sky: Café Sky is a well-liked place to have breakfast or lunch since it offers breathtaking rooftop views of Antigua's buildings and volcanoes. Delicious breakfast burritos, sandwiches, and fruit smoothies are all on the menu here.

b) Restaurante Hector's: Both residents and visitors like Restaurante Hector's for its traditional Guatemalan cuisine. For a memorable dining experience, I strongly suggest their Pepián and Kak'ik.

c) Sobremesa: Offering a superb dining experience with an emphasis on locally sourced and seasonal ingredients, Sobremesa gives a modern spin on classic cuisine. Their tasting meals provide the greatest tastes of Guatemala in a classy atmosphere.

d) Rainbow Café: This diverse eatery offers a variety of Western and Guatemalan foods on its worldwide menu. It's the perfect place to unwind after a day of exploring thanks to live music performances and a laid-back atmosphere.

Sweets from the Street

Examining Antigua's street food scene is a necessity if you want to fully experience the local culinary tradition. The following are some delicious street foods you should try:

Tostadas are a tasty and inexpensive snack made of crisp tortillas topped with guacamole, refried beans, shredded cabbage, and your choice of meat or veggies.

a) Elotes and Esquites: Enjoy grilled corn on the cob (elotes) or corn kernels served in a cup (esquites) with mayonnaise, cheese, chili powder, and lime juice on top.

b) Rellenitos de Plátano: These delicious plantain-filled snacks can be purchased at markets and street vendors and make the ideal dessert to consume on the move.

c) Garnachas: These little fried tortillas are topped with salsa, meat, and cabbage, much like tostadas.

d) Chuchitos: These little, packed maize masa dumplings are encased in a corn husk and resemble miniature tamales.

A fascinating trip through the tastes and customs of Guatemala may be experienced by investigating the eating and cuisine of Antigua. Every gastronomic experience in Antigua is a celebration of the nation's unique cultural history, whether it be enjoying regional specialties like Pepián and Kak'ik or exploring the buzzing street food scene. Whether you choose to eat in a nice restaurant or prefer the straightforward joys of street food, Antigua's sumptuous and unique tastes will leave you with a lifelong admiration for Guatemalan food.

Chapter 5: Outdoor Activities and Adventure: Exploring Guatemala's Natural Beauty

For nature lovers and adventure seekers alike, Guatemala, a nation rich in different landscapes and natural treasures, provides a variety of exhilarating outdoor activities and adventure options. Guatemala delivers an amazing experience for every adventurer, from climbing and trekking through lush woods and historic ruins to scaling mountains and enjoying the therapeutic hot springs. We shall examine some of the most thrilling outdoor pursuits and adventure possibilities the nation has to offer in this post.

Possibilities for Hiking and Trekking

With a variety of hiking and trekking trails to suit all ability levels, Guatemala is a hiker's delight. There are several possibilities to explore the country's diverse landscape, including its spectacular mountains, cloud forests, and lush jungles. The journey to the Mayan ruins of Tikal, where hikers may see breathtaking vistas of ancient temples towering from the rainforest canopy, is one of the most well-known hiking paths.

The Acatenango Overnight Hike is a well-liked choice for people looking for more difficult hikes. One of Guatemala's tallest volcanoes, Acatenango stands at a height of around 13,045 feet (3,976 meters) above sea level. The nighttime trip entails a strenuous climb, but the payoff is a breathtaking view of the eruptions of the nearby active Fuego Volcano beneath a sky full of stars. It is certainly a once-in-a-lifetime experience to see molten lava streaming down the slopes of Fuego.

Volcano Climbing and an Overnight Hike in Acatenango

Many outdoor enthusiasts go to Guatemala to participate in the unique thrill of volcano climbing. The Pacaya Volcano is yet another well-liked vacation spot in addition to Acatenango. Since Pacaya is one of the easiest to reach volcanoes, hikers may safely see lava flows there. This trek is remarkable because of the exhilaration of stepping on volcanic ash and seeing the flaming sight up close.

When climbing volcanoes, safety is always a top consideration, thus it is crucial to go with knowledgeable experts who are acquainted with the local geography and climate. Because volcanoes are inherently unpredictable, experienced guides make sure that tourists have a fun and safe journey.

tours of coffee plantations

The coffee plantation excursions offered in Guatemala are a sensory delight for anyone looking for a more laid-back outdoor experience. Coffee farming has always played a vital role in Guatemala's economy and culture. Visitors are welcome to stroll around the verdant coffee farms, see how the beans are grown and harvested, and even take part in the preparation of a cup of coffee.

A UNESCO World Heritage Site, Antigua is known for its coffee tours and is home to some of the best coffee farms in the nation. The trips often end with a pleasant coffee tasting so guests may experience the distinctive tastes of Guatemalan coffee and get a greater understanding of this well-liked brew.

Steam baths and hot springs

A trip to one of Guatemala's hot springs or thermal baths is the ideal way to unwind and revitalize after a day of climbing and touring.

Because of its volcanic activity, the nation offers a number of geothermal locations that provide relaxing and healing hot springs.

One of the most well-known hot springs is Fuentes Georginas, which is close to Quetzaltenango. These natural hot springs, which are surrounded by thick woods, create a tranquil atmosphere that lets tourists relax and bathe in the mineral-rich waters while admiring the lovely surroundings.

Canopy tours and zip-lining

Guatemala's zip-lining and canopy excursions provide an amazing experience high above the trees for adrenaline junkies and adventure seekers. Because of the nation's extensive rainforests and varied flora and wildlife, zip-lining is an exhilarating opportunity to see the natural beauty from a different angle.

Many zip-lining trips also feature platforms and suspension bridges that let people move through the treetops, giving them the opportunity to see different bird species and other animals. These trips are an incredible experience because of the exhilarating rush and the magnificent scenery.

A broad variety of interests and preferences are catered for by Guatemala's outdoor activities and adventure opportunities. Guatemala offers something exceptional to offer, regardless of whether you are an experienced hiker, an enthusiastic volcano climber, a coffee connoisseur, or someone looking for exhilarating adventures like zip-lining.

Always place safety and environmental sensitivity as top priorities while exploring the nation's natural beauties. In addition to enhancing your journey, guided excursions with knowledgeable guides will make sure that you have a good influence on the nearby ecosystems and communities. Take on an adventurous mindset, acquaint yourself with Guatemala's marvels, and make lifelong experiences.

Chapter 6: Immersion in Cultural and Artistic Experiences

Humanity's legacy is inextricably linked to cultural and creative experiences, which provide insight into various customs, creativity, and expression. Numerous chances exist in 2023 to visit and interact with regional art galleries, traditional crafts, and exciting events. These encounters not only enable travelers to explore the creative world but also provide a greater comprehension of a region's rich cultural heritage. This article emphasizes the value and attractiveness of going to nearby art galleries, taking part in local artisan classes, and experiencing the thrill of festivals and events in 2023.

Visiting regional galleries of art

The beliefs, viewpoints, and history of a town are captured in art galleries, which act as windows into its spirit. Visitors have a rare opportunity to engage with a community's cultural pulse and see the artistic prowess of local artists by perusing local art galleries. A historical gallery or a modern art venue both provide a wide variety of visual encounters that arouse feelings and spark contemplation.

Numerous art exhibits including both well-known and up-and-coming artists are set to take place in 2023 in various cities and towns. Art lovers could expect immersive exhibitions of mixed-media, photography, sculpture, and paintings. Local galleries often plan exhibits on particular topics that provide visitors the chance to learn in-depth about social challenges, environmental difficulties, or cultural history.

These galleries provide more than simply the chance to enjoy art. One may learn more about the creative process, the inspiration for the works of art, and the messages they express by interacting with artists and curators. Additionally, some galleries may provide guided tours, seminars, and art discussions to help visitors better understand and appreciate the artwork on show.

Traditional Workshops and Crafts

For the sake of preserving a region's cultural identity and legacy, traditional crafts must be preserved. In 2023, traditional craft studios provide visitors a rare chance to study under accomplished craftspeople and see the technique up close. These programs often take place in charming towns, historical landmarks, or cultural hubs, giving participants access to a rich and genuine atmosphere.

Workshops that teach crafts including ceramics, weaving, woodworking, metalworking, and folk art may be found all around the globe. The skills, background, and cultural value of these crafts will be taught to participants, ensuring that the information is preserved for future generations.

Traditional craft programs help people develop their creativity, patience, and feeling of achievement. Making something with one's hands gives one a special feeling of fulfillment and links them to their hosts' long-standing customs. Supporting these workshops promotes not just personal growth but also local economic sustainability and the ability of craftsmen to carry on their customs.

Calendar of Festivals and Events 2023

The culture, morals, and beliefs of a community are vividly reflected in its festivals. A broad variety of celebrations and events will take place all around the globe in 2023, each of which will be exciting for both residents and visitors.

cultural celebrations

Visitors may immerse themselves in a region's traditions and culture via cultural festivals. These gatherings highlight the vivid variety of other cultures via music, dancing, traditional food, and traditions. For instance, some of the most well-known cultural festivals that bring visitors from all over the world include the Chinese New Year festivities, the Holi Festival in India, and the Rio Carnival in Brazil.

Artist Festivals

Art festivals in 2023 provide a singular venue for artists to display their creations and promote innovative encounters with the general audience. Live performances, art installations, seminars, and interactive displays are often included at these events. The Venice Biennale in Italy, Burning Man in the United States, and Art Basel in Switzerland are notable examples.

Festivals of music

In 2023, fans of all types of music may attend a plethora of festivals. Everyone may find something they like, whether they prefer classical music, jazz, rock, electronic music, or global music. Festivals with stellar lineups and immersive experiences include Tomorrowland in Belgium, Coachella in the United States, and Glastonbury in the United Kingdom.

Reading Festivals

Literary festivals are a shelter for book enthusiasts to appreciate the written word. Author presentations, book launches, seminars, and panel discussions are often included in these events. The Hay Festival in Wales, the Jaipur Literature Festival in India, and the Edinburgh International Book Festival in Scotland are a few renowned literary events.

An stimulating voyage of inquiry, comprehension, and enjoyment of many customs, creativity, and expressions is provided through 2023's cultural and creative experiences. While traditional artisan workshops maintain traditions and encourage creativity, visiting local art galleries allows tourists to experience the essence of a town via art. Participating in festivals and events allows one to experience the delight of a large-scale celebration of culture and creativity. Let's take advantage of these chances to engage with the cultural richness of the globe and support the preservation of creative legacy for future generations as tourists and aficionados.

Chapter 7: Entertainment and Nightlife

People looking to relax, mingle, and have fun when the sun goes down can find a wide variety of activities in the thriving world of nightlife and entertainment. In this investigation, we focus on nightclubs and dancing, live music venues, and bars and pubs as three essential components of the nighttime scene. These places of entertainment have long served as the center of urban culture, offering areas for celebration, unwinding, and creative expression. Nightlife is a crucial component of modern urban living since each category provides distinctive experiences that appeal to various interests and preferences.

Pubs and bars

Nightlife would not be complete without bars and pubs, which provide a comfortable and laid-back ambiance in which customers may partake of a variety of alcoholic drinks, finger foods, and interesting discussions. These places often feature distinctive themes, furnishings, and specialty beverages, which add to their unique character. While some pubs may embrace modern aesthetics with a contemporary design, others may embrace a traditional, old-world vibe with low lighting and antique furnishings.

The main draw of bars and pubs is their social atmosphere. Customers may socialize with both friends and strangers, promoting a feeling of unity and belonging. Numerous bars also have themed evenings, quiz contests, or open mic nights, providing possibilities for entertainment more than just drinking.

Rooftop bars, which provide breath-taking views of the metropolis as guests drink cocktails beneath the stars, are becoming more and more common in major cities. Additionally, speakeasies have made a comeback, concealed behind inconspicuous facades, lending a sense of exclusivity and mystery to the nighttime experience.

Live Music Locations

Live music venues are a refuge for creative expression and creativity for music lovers. These venues are home to gifted musicians, bands, and performers that put on engaging shows in a variety of genres, such as rock, jazz, blues, hip-hop, and more. From cozy settings like cafés and tiny clubs to spacious concert halls and outdoor amphitheaters, live music venues come in different shapes and sizes.

Live music venues provide an electrifying energy that is contagious, causing the crowd to move to the beat and applaud for their favorite musicians. Concerts often include sophisticated stage designs, eye-catching light displays, and top-notch audio systems that improve the whole experience.

Famous towns with thriving live music cultures, like Nashville, Austin, and New Orleans, draw visitors and music fans from all over the globe. Live music performances have become more diverse and varied in many locations because to the rise of local bands and independent musicians.

Clubs at night and dancing

Nightclubs are often associated with vibrant, energized nightlife. The atmosphere of the night is established by DJs or live electronic music performances at these establishments, which appeal to individuals looking for a dynamic and immersive experience. Large dance floors, cutting-edge lighting, and pounding tunes are common features of nightclubs, which keep the throng dancing into the wee hours of the morning.

Popular themed dance parties encourage attendees to dress up in accordance with a particular period, style, or idea. Numerous nightclubs also offer guest performances or invite well-known DJs, bringing large audiences from all over the world.

An avenue for self-expression and emancipation is provided by the dancing scene in nightclubs. As they dance to the music, people from many origins and cultures join together to enjoy it.

Urban culture is not complete without nightlife and entertainment, with a concentration on Bars and Pubs, Live Music Venues, Nightclubs, and Dancing. Each category provides a distinctive range of experiences that appeal to a broad range of interests and preferences. While live music venues provide musicians a stage to perform and forge deeper connections with their listeners, bars and pubs foster a pleasant atmosphere that promotes social interaction. On the other side, nightclubs enliven the evening with exhilarating energy, luring people to the dance floor to celebrate music and life.

With cutting-edge ideas, transient venues, and cultural fusion, nightlife and entertainment are continuing to change the urban environment. The nightlife culture develops and changes as cities grow and diversity, becoming one of their defining characteristics.

The appeal of nightlife continues to be a continual pull for city inhabitants and tourists alike, whether it's a calm night at a lovely pub, an amazing live music performance, or an intense dance party. The pull of nightlife and entertainment calls as the sun sets and the city lights flood the streets, promising a night full of wonderful experiences and memories.

Chapter 8: Relaxation and Wellness

Finding strategies to obtain health and relaxation in today's fast-paced world is crucial for preserving one's physical, mental, and emotional well-being. Yoga and meditation studios, as well as spas and health retreats, are two of the most well-liked places where people may find solace from the strains of everyday life. In this article, we will go into the realms of health and relaxation, putting particular emphasis on these two practices, examining their advantages, and figuring out why they have become so widely accepted.

Centers for meditation and yoga

The ancient traditions of India and other countries are where yoga and meditation first appeared. Yoga promotes physical flexibility, strength, and inner tranquility by combining physical postures, breathing exercises, and meditation practices. Meditation centers have become established locations where people may practice mindfulness exercises including meditation and other mindfulness methods.

Origins and theory: The Yoga Sutras, a foundational literature that describes the theory and practices of yoga, were written by the ancient Indian philosopher Patanjali. This is where yoga's origins may be found. In order to develop peace and self-awareness, it promotes the integration of the body, mind, and spirit.

Yoga provides significant health advantages, as has been scientifically shown. Regular practice helps lessen tension and anxiety while improving posture, flexibility, and balance. Additionally, it improves cardiovascular health and muscular strength. People who meditate often report having lower blood pressure and better attention.

Environment and Community: Yoga and meditation studios foster a feeling of neighborhood among its patrons. People of all ages and abilities may congregate there to learn and develop in a welcoming, inclusive atmosphere. These facilities' atmosphere, which is often ornamented with calming accents and peaceful settings, aids in promoting peace and tranquillity.

Wellness retreats and spas

Spas and wellness retreats are becoming more and more well-liked as people want to unwind from their hectic life and partake in revitalizing activities. These businesses provide a variety of holistic activities, health services, and relaxation techniques to enhance general wellbeing.

Spas and wellness retreats are created to provide a tranquil and opulent atmosphere where visitors may rest and revitalize. The range of services, which cater to both physical and emotional relaxation, ranges from calming massages to energizing facials and body treatments.

Wellness retreats often take a holistic approach to wellbeing, taking into account the interdependence of the mind, body, and spirit. In addition to customary spa services, they could include dietary advice, mindfulness seminars, yoga and meditation sessions, and nature walks to help clients lead healthy lives.

Healing and detoxifying are major themes at many health retreats. Some provide specific detoxification programs, either via specially designed diets or natural treatments like hydrotherapy or saunas. These techniques support mental clarity and emotional recovery in addition to physical well-being.

The Increasing Popularity of Relaxation and Wellness Techniques

Stress and contemporary Life: The fast-paced, technologically-driven lifestyle of the contemporary world has a negative impact on health by raising stress levels. In order to find peace and relaxation among the commotion, individuals are turning to health disciplines like yoga, meditation, and spa getaways.

Media and Celebrity Endorsements: The popularity of wellness practices has also been aided by the growth of social media and celebrity endorsements. Influential people freely discuss their advantages and experiences, inspiring their followers to investigate these methods.

Recognition by the Medical Community: Wellness practices' acceptability and incorporation into society as a whole have been facilitated by the medical community's recognition of the beneficial effects of these practices. Yoga, meditation, and relaxation exercises are often suggested by doctors and other healthcare professionals as supplementary therapy to enhance general health.

In conclusion, wellness and relaxation techniques have become crucial resources for sustaining a balanced and healthy lifestyle in the busy world of today. Centers for yoga and meditation provide a setting for self-reflection and self-awareness, fostering both physical and mental health. While stressing a comprehensive approach to general health, spas and wellness retreats provide a haven for rest and renewal. These techniques are becoming more and more common because of their established health advantages, the need for stress alleviation, and the medical community's awareness of their importance. Individuals may acquire a feeling of peace and lead full lives by adopting health and relaxation techniques.

Chapter 9: Practical Travel Advice

Exploring new cultures, cuisines, and landscapes may be a rewarding and thrilling experience that comes with travel. However, in order to guarantee safe, fun, and responsible travel, it is crucial to be well-prepared and educated. We will concentrate on practical travel advice in this book, including advice on health and safety, local etiquette and traditions, and sustainable travel practices.

Security and Safety

Before leaving on your vacation, do a substantial amount of research about your location. Recognize the political climate, laws, and traditions of the area. To be informed about security issues, look for travel warnings issued by your government.

Register with your Embassy: Inform the embassy or consulate of your country in the nation where you want to go. In the event of an emergency or crisis, communication will be facilitated by this.

Invest in comprehensive travel insurance that can protect you against unexpected circumstances like lost luggage and medical crises.

Protect your Property: Store your valuables, such as passports, cash, and devices, in a safe and secret place. Use a locked bag or a money belt, if possible.

Avoid Flashy Displays: To reduce the chance of theft, stay away from putting valuable things on show in busy areas, such as jewelry, cameras, or gadgets.

Aware of your surroundings is especially important in crowded tourist locations, on public transit, and in busy streets. Be watchful for scams and pickpockets.

Know Local Emergency Numbers: Store your embassy's contact details as well as police, hospital, and other local emergency numbers on your phone.

Share Itinerary: Let a family member or friend who you trust know where you'll be going so they may contact you in an emergency.

Avoid Risky regions: Tourists may encounter risky regions in every location. Keep yourself informed and stay out of these risky areas.

Safety in transportation: Whether using a cab, using a ride-sharing service, or using public transit, choose reliable and authorized solutions. Always use a seatbelt while driving.

Medical and Health Information

Visit your doctor for a health checkup before your trip to discuss immunizations, prescriptions, and any possible health hazards in the area.

Make sure you have the appropriate travel immunizations and health documents for your intended location. Certain vaccines may need to be documented in certain countries.

Prescription Drugs: Always have a sufficient amount of prescription drugs on hand, as well as a copy of the prescription and the drugs' generic names.

First aid materials such as bandages, antiseptic creams, painkillers, antihistamines, and any necessary prescription drugs should be included in your travel first aid box.

Food and Water Safety: under areas where the quality of the water is under doubt, consume bottled water instead of ice-filled beverages. Avoid eating from carts and choose hot, prepared meals instead.

Use insect repellent and wear protective clothes to ward against mosquito and pest bites, particularly in places where dengue or malaria are a risk.

Keep Hydrated: To prevent dehydration, drink lots of water, particularly in hot and humid areas.

Sun protection: To shield oneself from the sun's damaging UV rays, use sunscreen, sunglasses, and a wide-brimmed hat.

To lessen the symptoms of jet lag while traveling across many time zones, adapt your sleep routine before departure and drink enough water.

Medical Facilities: Become familiar with the locations of the hospitals and medical facilities at your destination.

Local Customs and Etiquette

Learn a Few fundamental Local words: To communicate more effectively and demonstrate respect, learn a few fundamental words in the local tongue.

Respect the local clothing code, particularly in conservative areas or at religious locations.

Know the regional practices for welcoming people. Handshakes, bows, and cheek kisses may be suitable in various cultures.

Table Manners: Be aware of regional table manners and eating traditions since they might differ greatly from one nation to the next.

Respectful behavior is expected while visiting religious and cultural places. Dress modestly and observe any rituals or restrictions that may apply.

Asking for permission before taking pictures of people is always polite, particularly in delicate situations or private locations.

When giving presents, keep in mind cultural standards and steer clear of anything that can be seen as rude or unsuitable.

Research the different tipping cultures across the world. Tipping may be considered impolite in certain locations while it may be required in others.

Regarding personal space, keep in mind that various cultures may have differing degrees of comfort with close physical contact.

Respect Local rules: Adhere to local rules and ordinances, especially if they diverge from customs in your native nation.

Green Travel Advice

Bring a reusable water bottle and shopping bag to reduce the amount of single-use plastic trash.

Support Local Communities: To help the community's economy, choose locally owned hotels, eateries, and tour companies.

Respect wildlife by not disturbing or feeding it while you observe it in its natural environment.

Avoid practices that might hurt or exploit animals.

Save Water and Energy: Use resources wisely, and choose eco-friendly lodging that puts sustainability first.

Buy souvenirs that are ethically sourced, do not affect the environment, or do not harm endangered animals.

Use Public Transportation: To cut down on carbon emissions, take the bus, walk, or ride your bike more often.

Keep to authorized Trails and routes: To prevent harming sensitive ecosystems, keep to authorized trails and routes.

Reduce Plastic garbage: Steer clear of single-use plastics and properly dispose of garbage, recycling where practical.

Cultural Sensitivity: Be mindful of regional norms and traditions and only engage in authentic, respectful cultural encounters.

Volunteer Responsibly: If you decide to give back to the local community while on your vacation, choose trustworthy organizations that do it in a long-lasting and beneficial way.

In conclusion, the keys to successful and happy travel are planning, awareness, and respect. You may maximize your trip and positively impact the areas you visit by following these useful travel advice for safety and security, health and medical information, local manners and traditions, and sustainable travel practices. Never forget that being a responsible traveler not only protects your safety but also contributes to the preservation and protection of our world's beauty and variety for future generations to discover and enjoy.

Chapter 10: Day Trips from Antigua: Discovering Guatemala's Diverse Beauty

With its well-preserved Spanish Baroque-influenced architecture and dynamic culture, Antigua, Guatemala, is a mesmerizing city. It is the ideal starting point for tourists seeking to go on interesting day excursions to experience the country's varied natural beauties since it is nestled in the highlands. In this trip, we'll explore Guatemala City, Lake Atitlán, Chichicastenango Market, and Pacaya Volcano National Park, four fascinating places close to Antigua.

Where Modernity Meets Tradition in Guatemala City

Guatemala City, the nation's capital and biggest city, is just 45 minutes away from Antigua.

Guatemala City has its own distinctive charms, although sometimes being eclipsed by Antigua's attractiveness. The city skillfully combines its deeply ingrained indigenous traditions with modernity.

Start your adventure with the National Palace, a magnificent architectural marvel that houses the government's offices and a stunning collection of murals that chronicle the history of the country.

La Aurora Zoo: One of the most well-known zoos in Central America, La Aurora Zoo offers a range of exotic animals in a verdant setting for a family-friendly experience.

Ixchel Museum: Explore traditional textiles and discover the workmanship of indigenous people as you delve into Guatemala's Mayan legacy at the Ixchel Museum of Indigenous Textiles and Clothing.

Visit the Central Market, a lively center where you can buy a variety of traditional handicrafts, fresh vegetables, and delectable street cuisine, to immerse yourself in the local culture.

The Pearl of the Guatemalan Highlands is Lake Atitlan.

Awe-inspiring Lake Atitlán, located just a few hours from Antigua, is encircled by three towering volcanoes and charming indigenous settlements. The tranquil beauty of this lake, one of the most stunning in the world, will wow you.

Start your day in the bustling lakeshore community of Panajachel. Take a leisurely stroll along Santander Street, which is packed with stores and eateries, and don't pass up the chance to go on a boat excursion to see the local towns.

San Juan La Laguna is a center for the arts and is well-known for its burgeoning art scene and traditional Mayan culture. Here, you can see how local weavers create vibrant fabrics and see how natural coloring works.

Santiago Atitlán is a lovely lakeside community that provides an intriguing fusion of Catholic and Mayan customs. Visit the Maximón sanctuary, where the indigenous people worship a unique divinity, and explore the neighborhood markets.

Indian Nose hike: If you're looking for a little excitement, think about making the ascent to the Indian Nose viewpoint. Trekkers who go out early in the morning are rewarded with breathtaking dawn views of the lake and the mountains that surround it.

Market in Chichicastenango: A Rainbow of Colors and Traditions

To see the colorful Chichicastenango Market, one of the most well-known marketplaces in Central America, travel for approximately two hours from Antigua. The market, which takes place on Thursdays and Sundays, is a dazzling display of regional customs, noises, and colors.

Experience the market by meandering through the labyrinth of booths selling anything from handmade ceramics and fresh fruit to colorful fabrics and locally grown medicinal herbs. Engage with local sellers to hone your negotiating skills.

Santo Tomás Church: The stunning Santo Tomás Church is located within the market, where you can see the remarkable fusion of Catholic rituals and Mayan rites during religious celebrations.

Visit Pascual Abaj, a historic stone structure formerly utilized for Mayan rites and ceremonies, for a fuller understanding of indigenous spiritual traditions.

National Park of the Pacaya Volcano: A Fiery Adventure

Pacaya Volcano National Park makes for an exciting day excursion for nature enthusiasts and adventurers. This active volcano, which is just one hour from Antigua, offers tourists the chance to see lava flows and get a sense of nature's untamed strength.

Volcano climb: Set off on a guided climb up the volcano, through lava fields and volcanic vistas. You'll be rewarded for climbing with beautiful views of the surroundings.

Observe the red-hot lava flows in astonishment as you watch them from a safe distance. Observing the molten core of the planet in motion is a strange experience.

Marshmallow Roasting: A spectacular experience you won't find anywhere else, roast marshmallows over the volcano's geothermal heat for a special treat.

Antigua, Guatemala, is a starting point for exploring a world of varied natural beauty and cultural diversity. Each day journey provides a distinctive and enlightening experience, from the sophistication of Guatemala City to the calm serenity of Lake Atitlán, the brilliant colors of Chichicastenango Market, and the fiery adventure of Pacaya Volcano National Park. Put on your explorer's hat, grab your baggage, and go off to explore the fascinating natural beauties that surround this historic city.

Language & Phrases Guide for Daily Use

Welcome to Antigua, Guatemala, a city renowned for its thriving culture, magnificent architecture, and spectacular natural surroundings. Effective communication with the locals will enhance your experience as you set out on your adventure through this historical treasure. To assist you in navigating Antigua's streets and fully experiencing its distinctive charm, we have provided you with a complete list of handy sayings and a linguistic guide in this travel guide.

Simple Greetings and Compliments
Begin every conversation with a courteous and welcoming hello. Since Spanish is the official language of Guatemala, knowing a few basic phrases would be quite helpful.

"Hola" (Hello) is a short, common greeting appropriate for all situations.

Use "Buenos das" (Good morning) from early in the morning till noon.

"Buenas tardes" (good afternoon) is the appropriate greeting for the late afternoon and early evening.

When greeting someone after nightfall, say "Buenas noches" (good evening/night).

What's going on? Do you feel well? - A joking method of inquiring about someone's wellbeing.

Express your gratitude by saying "gracias" (thank you) for any assistance or service you have received.

How to Get Around the City

A few key words for transportation and instructions are necessary for navigating Antigua:

What does it cost? (How much is it going to cost?) - Useful for haggling with sellers or cab drivers about costs.

Where is it exactly? (Where am I?) - Type the address you're looking for, such as a landmark or a restaurant.
"Can you help me, Voy a?" (I'm about to... can you assist me?) - When trying to locate a particular location, ask for help.

How did you get there? How can I reach...? - Obtain instructions to a location you want to visit.

Place a Food and Drink Order

A delicious selection of regional cuisine is available in Antigua. To enjoy the food of the area, say the following:

Please, a table for a certain number of people. (A table for [number] persons, please) - Make a restaurant reservation.

"I'd like to order..." (I'd want to place a... Prior to mentioning the meal you want, use this statement.

"Pretty please, a beer" (May I have a beer? - Grab a local beer to rehydrate

"La cuenta, please" When you're prepared to make a payment, say, "The bill, please."

Crisis Situations

Despite the fact that Antigua is typically secure, it is important to be ready for unanticipated circumstances:

In an emergency, say "Ayuda" (Help) to request help.
"Necesito un médico" (I need a doctor) indicates that you should seek care if necessary.
"Where is the police station?" (Where is the police department located? - Ask where the closest police station is.

Negotiating and Shopping

In Antigua, you must visit the marketplaces. The following words can help you while you shop:

What does this cost? (How much is it going to cost?) - Request information about an item's pricing.

"Es muy caro" means "it's too expensive." - If you think the price is too high, kindly try to negotiate.

Could you please give me a discount? Please offer me a discount. - When haggling with merchants, ask for a discount.

How to Be Thankful and Polite

Guatemalan culture places a great value on politeness. Use these words to express respect:

When making requests or requesting assistance, use "por favor" (please).

To gain someone's attention or to apologize for interrupting, say "disculpe" (excuse me).

Ask for permission before entering someone's home or personal space by using the term "permiso" (permission).

Making Friends and Developing Relationships

Make relationships and enduring experiences by interacting with the community:

What is your name, please? How may I address you? - Start discussions by becoming familiar with names.

"Enchanted to meet you" (Good to see you.) - Let them know how happy you are to meet them.

Would you want to be my friend? You want to be my buddy, right? - Invite a local in a kind manner.

Congratulations! You're well-prepared to discover Antigua, Guatemala's treasures with the help of this extensive collection of practical sayings and a linguistic guide. Keep in mind that language is the key to gaining access to cultural experiences and developing deep relationships with the individuals you meet. Take part in the unique traditions of the community, savor the mouthwatering food, and learn about the fascinating history of this beautiful city. Warmth and generosity from the welcoming Guatemalan inhabitants will surely make your trip to Antigua memorable. Good travels! (Enjoy your journey!)

Conclusion

As a result, Antigua, Guatemala, is a world-class tourism destination that mesmerizes visitors with its rich past, lively culture, and magnificent scenery. In our comprehensive travel guide to Antigua, Guatemala for 2023, we've examined the city's finest sights, unique experiences, lodging possibilities, and adventurous activities, making it a genuinely remarkable trip for all kinds of tourists.

Accepting Culture and History:

Antigua is a site where the past and present collide, and its historical importance permeates the whole city. The city's well-preserved colonial buildings, cobblestone streets, and historic ruins transport tourists back in time with a nostalgic feeling. A look into the city's colonial history and the lasting spirit of the Guatemalan people may be had by seeing sites like the Santa Catalina Arch, San Jose Cathedral, and Convent of the Capuchins.

Antigua's vibrant festivals, busy markets, and unique crafts all contribute to the island's outstanding cultural legacy. By visiting the Central Market, mingling with the welcoming inhabitants, and taking part in customary festivals like Semana Santa, the Holy Week holiday, tourists may fully immerse themselves in the local way of life. The people of Guatemala are friendly and kind, and this makes tourists feel at home and welcome throughout their whole stay.

Pleasant Culinary Experiences

The cuisine of Antigua is a fascinating blend of Spanish and local Mayan tastes. The city is a delight for food lovers, with everything from street vendors selling delicious tamales and chuchitos to fine-dining restaurants serving sophisticated takes on classic meals. Travelers may experience delicious chocolate delicacies, traditional Guatemalan coffee, and regional cuisine like Pepián and Rellenitos.

In addition to being a feast for the taste sensations, exploring the city's culinary scene offers a window into the core of Guatemalan culture and customs. Every eating experience in Antigua is enlightening and fulfilling because of the gastronomic variety that represents the nation's history and ethnic background.

Choices for Comfy Accommodations:

To meet the requirements and tastes of every visitor, Antigua provides a wide selection of lodging choices. There are plenty of cozy places to stay, from modest boutique hotels tucked within colonial structures to cutting-edge luxury resorts with breathtaking views of the nearby volcanoes. The Antigua hotels and guesthouses are renowned for their friendly hospitality, attentive service, and commitment to giving visitors a genuine and immersive experience.

Antigua is the perfect destination for those looking for a luxury break, while explorers on a tight budget may stay in comfortable hostels without sacrificing comfort. Visitors are likely to discover a home away from home with any choice they choose, enabling them to unwind and recharge after days of travel and excitement.

Many Adventures:

Adventurers may enhance their trip experience with a variety of exhilarating activities available in Antigua. Acatenango or Pacaya are two neighboring volcanoes that are worth climbing for the stunning panoramic views and the possibility to see molten lava. Discovering the city's natural splendor while riding a horse or on a mountain bike adds an element of adventure.

In addition, the area's beautiful woods and clear lakes provide plenty of opportunity for hikers, birdwatchers, and nature lovers. Swimming at Santa Teresita's hot pools is an exhilarating and refreshing experience, making it a must-do activity when visiting Antigua.

Keeping Culture and the Environment Alive:

It is crucial for tourists to understand how their actions affect the places they visit. With its priceless historical landmarks and breathtaking natural surroundings, Antigua deserves tourism that is sustainable and responsible. The preservation of the city's culture, traditions, and ecology must be supported, as must local companies, craftsmen, and projects.

We can help preserve Antigua's beauty and make sure that future generations may appreciate this lovely city as much as we do by adhering to local traditions and reducing our environmental impact.

Guatemala's Antigua is a monument to the splendor of human history, culture, and exploration. It has plenty to offer every tourist with its rich historical attractions, thriving cultural scene, delectable food, cozy lodging alternatives, and adventurous attitude. As we say goodbye to this magical city, let's take with us the memories of its kind people, breathtaking scenery, and illustrious past. I hope the Antigua, Guatemala travel guide for 2023 arouses curiosity and encourages readers to go out on their own wonderful visit to this amazing location.

Printed in Great Britain
by Amazon

31842529R00050